A journey through time to
discover the incredible story of
how Zamzam came to be.

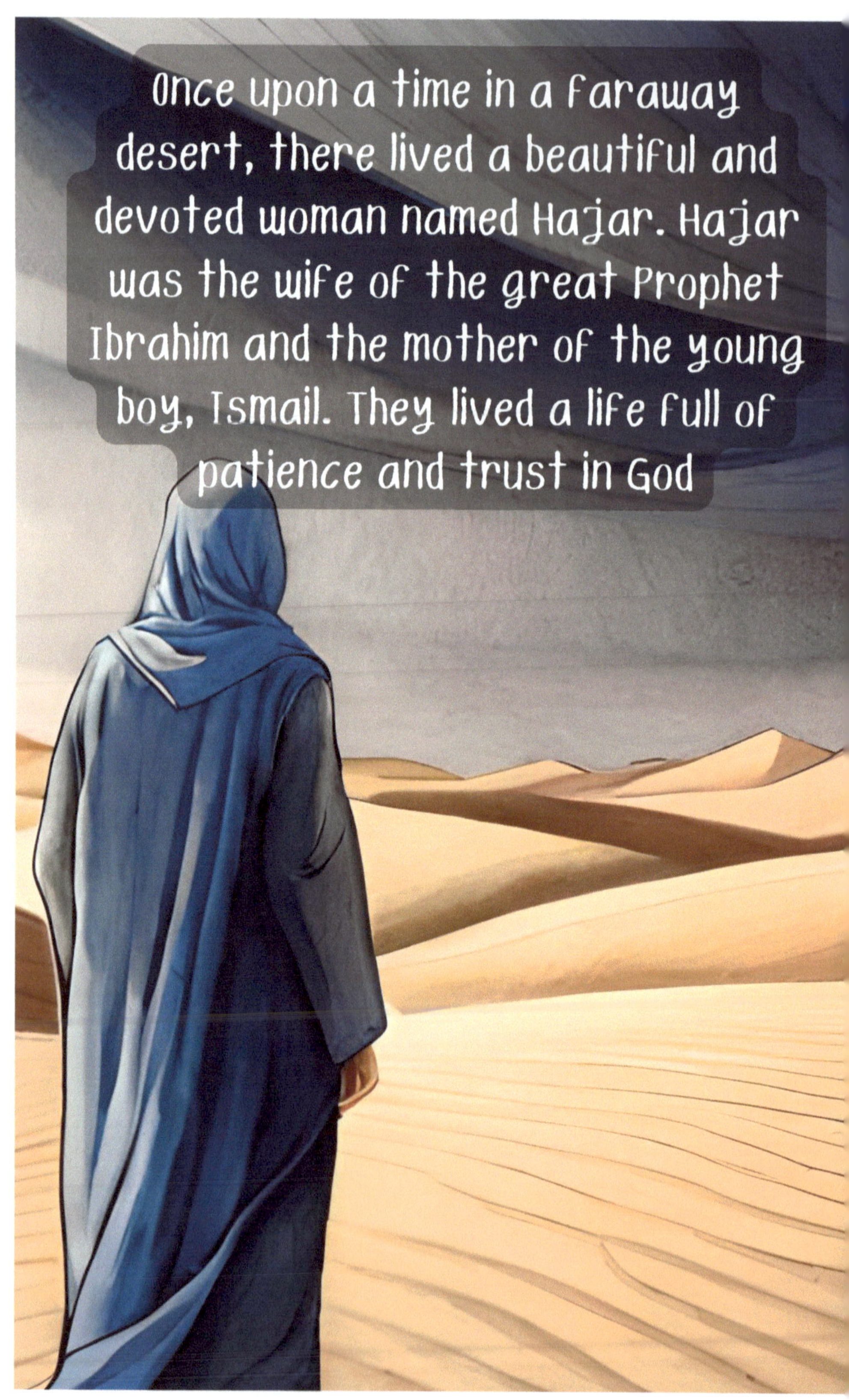

Once upon a time in a faraway desert, there lived a beautiful and devoted woman named Hajar. Hajar was the wife of the great Prophet Ibrahim and the mother of the young boy, Ismail. They lived a life full of patience and trust in God

One sunny day, Prophet Ibrahim was instructed by Allah to take Hajar and their baby Ismail to a distant, barren land. This land was completely empty, with no water or food to be found.

Hajar was quite reluctant to stay alone in the desert, but when she learnt that it was God's command, she put her trust in Allah and agreed to stay alone.

Before leaving both of them in the desert with some provisions, including the water skin and some dates, Ibrahim recited the following supplication:

رَّبَّنَا إِنِّي أَسْكَنتُ مِن ذُرِّيَّتِي بِوَادٍ غَيْرِ ذِي زَرْعٍ عِندَ بَيْتِكَ الْمُحَرَّمِ رَبَّنَا لِيُقِيمُوا الصَّلَاةَ فَاجْعَلْ أَفْئِدَةً مَّنَ النَّاسِ تَهْوِي إِلَيْهِمْ وَارْزُقْهُم مِّنَ الثَّمَرَاتِ لَعَلَّهُمْ يَشْكُرُونَ

"Our Lord, I have settled some of my descendants in an uncultivated valley near your sacred House, our Lord, that they may establish prayer. So make hearts among the people incline toward them and provide for them from the fruits that they might be grateful."
[Surah Ibrahim, 14:37]

As they reached this desolate place, Prophet Ibrahim left them with a small amount of food and water. He prayed to Allah to watch over them and provide them with sustenance.

And with that, he turned and walked away, leaving Hajar and Ismail alone in the vast desert.

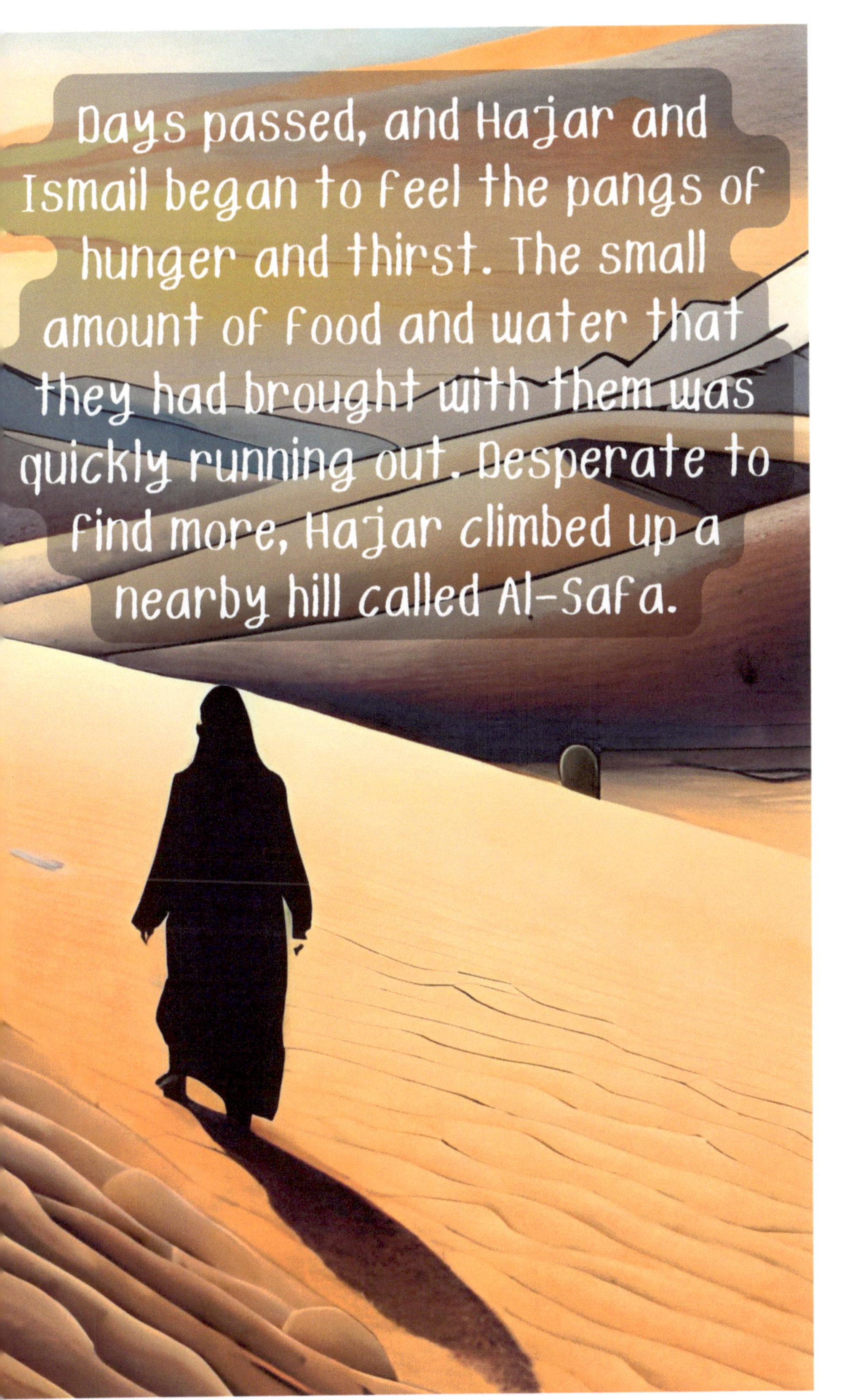

Days passed, and Hajar and Ismail began to feel the pangs of hunger and thirst. The small amount of food and water that they had brought with them was quickly running out. Desperate to find more, Hajar climbed up a nearby hill called Al-Safa.

From the top of Al-Safa, she scanned the horizon, hoping to glimpse a sign of water or a passing traveler who could help them. But all she could see was the endless desert, stretching out in every direction.

Not wanting to give up, Hajar decided to try another hill nearby called Al-Marwah. She raced down Al-Safa and across the sandy valley, her heart pounding with hope and fear.

As she reached the top of Al-Marwah, she again looked out across the desert, praying for a miracle. But once more, she was met with only the sight of the barren landscape.

Despite her growing despair, Hajar refused to give up. She believed in Allah's promise, and she knew that He would provide for her and her son. So, she ran back and forth between Al-Safa and Al-Marwah seven times, each time searching the horizon for a sign of help.

Exhausted and nearly out of hope, Hajar returned to Ismail, who was lying on the ground, weak from thirst. As she approached, she noticed something incredible: a spring of water had miraculously appeared right where Ismail had been kicking the sand!

and then she filled up her water-
skin with her hands. As she
scooped up the water, it
continued to flow, so she said
'Zome, zome', which meant 'Stop,
stop' – as she was worried the
water would run out!

Angel Jibril (as) said to her, 'Don't be afraid of being neglected, for this is the House of Allah which will be built by this boy and his father, and Allah never neglects his people' [Tafsir Ibn Kathir]. He thus reminded her that, no matter how long they remained in the desert, she could continue to have confidence that Allah would provide for her, just as He had sent her water when she had thought the ground was barren.

Hajar rushed to the spring and filled her container with the cool, life-giving water. She and Ismail drank deeply, their strength returning as the water quenched their thirst.

Word of this miracle spread quickly, and soon, people from all across the desert began to gather around mecca, With the water from Zamzam.

they were able to grow crops and build a thriving community.

Since that day, every pilgrim visiting Makkah for Umrah or Hajj has to complete the ritual of taking seven rounds back and forth between Safa and Marwa hills.

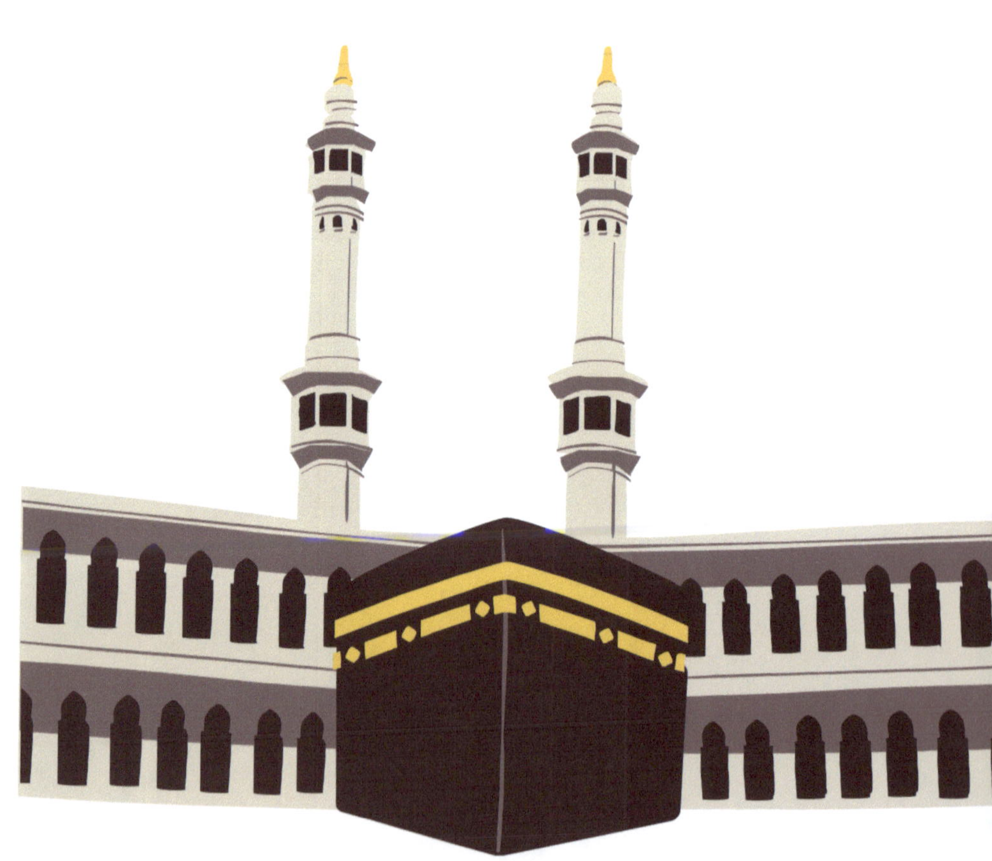

And so, the story of Hajar's faith and perseverance became a timeless tale for Muslims. Her brave journey between Al-Safa and Al-Marwah reminds us all that even in our darkest moments, if we place our trust in Allah, He will never abandon us.

Lessons from this Story of Hope

- Allah tests those that he loves. We have no doubt that the family of Ibrahim (as) were beloved to Allah, yet they experienced an incredibly painful situation. They were separated for many years, with Hajar (as) raising Ismail (as) alone in an uncultivated desert. This is a reminder to us that our own painful situations are tests which draw us closer to Allah, not signs that Allah has abandoned us.

Lessons from this Story of Hope

- Even if you can't find a solution, Allah will give you a way out. Hajar (as) ran between Safa and Marwa seven times, each time expecting to see a sign in the empty desert. Her absolute trust in Allah gave her certainty that He would send her a solution to a seemingly unsolvable problem.

Lessons from this Story of Hope

- Trust in Allah – but put in effort yourself. Hajar (as) could not trek across the desert until she found people, nor could she dig the barren ground until she struck water. There was little she could do in that situation to quench her baby's thirst. But she did not limit herself to only making du'a; she also made an effort to help herself, running to the top of two mountains to search for a sign of life.